Highballs
High Heels

a girl's guide to the art of cocktails

Highballs High

Karen Brooks, Gideon Bosker, and

Photographs by Mittie Hellmich

Heels

Reed Darmon

CHRONICLE BOOKS
SAN FRANCISCO

Library of Congress Cataloging-in-Publication Data:

Brooks, Karen.
       Highballs High Heels : a girl's guide to the art of
cocktails / by Karen Brooks, Gideon Bosker, and Reed
Darmon, with Mittie Hellmich.
            p.   cm.
       Includes index.
       ISBN 0-8118-3017-9
Cocktails. I. Bosker, Gideon. II. Darmon, Reed. III. Hellmich,
Mittie. IV. Title.

TX951 .B778324 2001
641.8'74—dc21   00-060352

Printed in Hong Kong.

Contemporary photos and styling by Mittie Hellmich
Designed by Reed Darmon

Distributed in Canada by Raincoast Books
9050 Shaughnessy Street
Vancouver, BC V6P 6E5

10 9 8 7 6 5 4 3 2

Chronicle Books LLC
85 Second Street
San Francisco, California 94105

www.chroniclebooks.com

dedication

To Ethel and Gert, Clara and Jodi,
Harriet and Lois, and Lynn and
Amy, whose love and loyalty
sparkle like fine Champagne.
— *Karen Brooks*

To J.D., who takes cocktails and
heels and turns them into music.
— *Gideon Bosker*

contents

Introduction

The making of a cocktail goddess

They said she could make music with her martini glass. Holding the delicate stem of her drink as a violinist would position her bow, our friend the Cocktail Goddess clinked a sleek, cone-shaped glass with so much grace and precision that it sounded like the clarified tinkle of a Balinese gamelan. It was an ear-tingling, resonant clink that said, "It doesn't get any better than this."

And in her presence, it didn't. Whether under the spell of her shimmering Cosmopolitan or a vodka martini twinkling with lemon rinds cut like stars, this much was undeniable: She made the place. Made it sing. She gave everyone a lesson in the refined pleasures that a cocktail hour could bring. Sometimes, under the spell of Herb Alpert's smooth rendition of the *Casino Royale* theme, she made the place come unglued.

A cocktail goddess, first and foremost, is a mood-maker and spell-caster. When a woman makes a drink, she becomes an epic force, a fearsome creature, with the power to dazzle and delight, command and control. She makes sure that her private theater is abuzz in lively, even mysterious, discourse. Silence is anathema to the empress of elixirs, so she must reign over the cocktail salon like a party shaman, pumping the house full of magically ornamented cocktails until the place is pulsating with conversation and conviviality. In her hands, a continuous stream of words fly through the air, ricocheting off people, glasses, and objects like the maniacal warbling of millions of birds.

A woman's cocktail domain can be torch, mod, or cool. It can be screen siren, tiki girl, or mondo bongo. Vivaldi and orchids. Solo days, girl-bonding weekends, or boy-toy nights. The range runs from Chambord-tinctured Champagne for a swank soiree to blood orange juice spiked with passion the morning after to a decadent milk shake laced with chocolate liqueur — the crème de la crème of hot-flash antidotes. It's the woman's call, because she is the alchemist extraordinaire, charged with blending spirits into potions that massage the spirit, mind, and body.

Just as every piece of clothing sends a silent message, so has every cocktail its purpose, its raison d'être. Some drinks make you smile, some make you think, some make you lazy, and others make you want to throw off your heels and take the step into uncharted territory.

Sometimes that territory is soul-wrenching emotional real estate, where a good drink is the only escape hatch from the tear-soaked nexus of unremitting heartache. As crooner Julie London put it in her famous song, "The Man Who Got Away": "A jigger of lying/garnished with fights/some bitters for crying/long unhappy nights/a dash of lost dream/then stir with regret/shake well and pour/then drink and forget."

Sometimes, of course, having a cocktail is not just a symbol of refinement, a cup of knowledge, or a glass of despair. It can simply

be a fun and wicked thing. If our gin-spiked Spy Girl cocktail gives you the courage to investigate your philandering boyfriend's credit card receipts, then our brandy-based Power Shower Punch might help you talk your best friend out of marrying the loser from Toledo with white belts and shoes. Hey, what's a good drink — or friend — for?

But attitude is only part of the package. Some cocktails simply transport you to a brighter, warmer world where every scintilla of pleasure is strobed, frozen, and suspended. Maybe it's Hot as Haiti, a glass of dark rum possessed with ginger brew, or Venus Envy, made with a legendary aphrodisiac liqueur that makes you feel every hot, sandy shiver, again and again; like a jungle fever that won't break until all the flickers have been fired. Have one on us.

And remember, style is as important as substance. When the spell-caster makes a drink, it should not only taste like ambrosia, it should look precious enough to be displayed in a window at Barneys'. After all, cocktails sparkling with a liquid rainbow of blue curaçao, green Midori, and pomegranate-red grenadine can turn a serving tray into a three-dimensional Miro painting.

Every cocktail has its time and place, and matching a drink with the appropriate occasion is key to earning status as a drink diva. For the heat of summer, the refreshing, aquamarine-colored Surfer Girl or the lean, green Bikinitini are customized for equatorial languor — or put simply, the beach. If you're getting even with the socialites you hated in high school, our Debutonics cocktail is perfectly placed among taffeta, falsies, and your sincerest fake smile. And finally, if there's one drink that says, "Baby, stop driving with the emergency brake on!," it would be the Armagnac-fueled Colette's Car.

In the end, cocktail culture for women is about dressing up or letting your hair down, having fun, entertaining with attitude, and taking control. There are many ways to get there. But as our friend the Cocktail Goddess likes to say, "The best highball is the one that makes you want to fling your heels high into the sky and say, 'I am woman, hear me pour.'"

— *Gideon Bosker and Karen Brooks*

Cool tools

The beauty of cocktail art is its simplicity. You don't need to buy expensive accessories or, worse, read how-to manuals. What you do need are some basic gadgets and gizmos, listed below, plus a sharp paring knife and a stash of plastic sword toothpicks or swank cocktail picks.

● **BAR SPOON:** The classic tool for stirring tall noncarbonated drinks and muddling ingredients is long and skinny, with a twisted handle and small spoon on one end.

● **CITRUS JUICER:** Fresh juice separates the pros from the dilettantes. An old-fashioned glass reamer or even a plastic one is perfect for the occasional drink, but an electric unit is ideal for frequent entertaining. Before juicing, roll and press the fruit on a flat surface or warm it under hot water to increase the juice yield.

● **COCKTAIL SHAKER:** As the market expands, you can go industrial, ultramod, or collectible, drawing from a wide range of options. The Boston shaker, preferred by bartenders

because it chills faster, contains a 16-ounce mixing glass and a slightly larger stainless steel cone that fastens upside-down over the glass; if you use one, you'll need to buy a separate spring-coil or Hawthorne strainer, designed to fit over the rim. The more stylish standard shaker contains a tumbler, built-in strainer, and fitted cap. Styles range from novelty shapes to Art Deco glass to high-tech versions with metal mesh casings.

● **ICE BUCKET:** The must-have glamour cocktail party accessory, complete with a set of metal tongs. Choices run from chic glass to stainless steel to colored plastic units. The ultimate splurge is the vacuum ice bucket, with a glass liner for insulation and a snug lid to keep ice from melting too quickly.

● **MIXING GLASS:** This is perfect for mixing martinis or more than two drinks at a time. Look for a 16-ounce glass with a pinched, molded lip to hold back the ice when you pour. As an alternative, use the glass of a Boston shaker and a Hawthorne strainer.

● MUDDLER: This rounded hardwood stick helps mash ingredients, crush herbs, or crack ice, though the end of a rounded rolling pin or a ceramic mortar and pestle will do.

● SHOT GLASS: Essential for measuring, shot glasses also are fun to collect.

● STIRRING ROD: The classic stir stick for martinis and Champagne drinks.

● SWIZZLE STICKS: Keep an assortment on hand for visuals, from campy numbers to unusual glass-blown shapes.

● ZESTER/STRIPPER: This tool is essential for garnishing. A vegetable peeler will do in a pinch, but it's clumsier and less precise.

mixer's measurements

	US	METRIC
Dash	1/8 oz	2 ml
Bar spoon	1/2 oz	15 ml
1 teaspoon	1/6 oz	5 ml
1 tablespoon (3 teaspoons)	1/2 oz	15 ml
2 tablespoons (pony)	1 fl oz	30 ml
3 tablespoons (jigger)	1 1/2 fl oz	45 ml
1/4 cup	2 fl oz	60 ml
1/3 cup	3 fl oz	80 ml
1/2 cup	4 fl oz	125 ml
2/3 cup	5 fl oz	160 ml
3/4 cup	6 fl oz	180 ml
1 cup	8 fl oz	250 ml
1 pint	16 fl oz	500 ml
1 quart	32 fl oz	1 liter

1 chocolate square = 4 tablespoons grated
1 medium lemon = 3 tablespoons juice
1 medium lime = 2 tablespoons juice
1 medium grapefruit = 2/3 cup juice
1 medium orange = 1/3 cup juice

Shake it, baby

Cocktail shaking, stirring drinks, and chilling glasses are all easy to master. Each requires just a few inside tips.

SHAKE LIKE A PRO:
If you are using a Boston shaker, fill it with cracked ice, preferably, or ice cubes. Turn the steel cone upside down and fit it snugly over the glass to form a seal. Grip both ends, keep the metal half on the bottom, and shake it vigorously up and down — when cold enough, your hands will stick to the shaker. Set the shaker down, glass side up. Push gently but firmly on one side to break the seal. Remove the glass. Fit a coil-spring strainer over the cone and strain the mixture into a serving glass. For a standard shaker, fill with ice, add the ingredients, and cap with the lid. Grip the neck, and place your index finger on the cap. Grip the bottom with your other hand, and shake briskly to blend and chill the ingredients. Strain through the built-in strainer.

SHAKING VS. STIRRING:
The rules of the game are simple. Stir drinks made of clear ingredients; shake drinks with juices, creams, and liqueurs. A stirred drink has a pristine beauty; a shaken one is cloudier.

TO CHILL A GLASS:
The shortcut method is to fill the glass with cracked ice and water and let it stand a few minutes — or pop the glass in the freezer for up to 10 minutes. Toss out the contents, shake out any excess water, and pour in the cocktail. For the perfect frosty glow, rinse the glass with cold water. Freeze at least 10 minutes and as long as overnight.

Ice girls

The best ice is made from filtered, spring, or bottled water. Some cocktail artists prefer ice cubes for stirring, shaking, and serving "on the rocks." Most swear by cracked ice, widely available in stores or made by placing cubes in a plastic bag covered with a cotton towel and gently cracking with a muddler or ice mallet.

Cool cubes

Decorative ice cubes add visual excitement to cocktails, and best of all, they can be made up to a week in advance. Which means more time for primping before the party.

- 14 ounces good-quality water or other liquid
- Ingredient to float in the center (See Variations)

1. Fill each cubicle of an ice cube tray half full of water. Place in the freezer until partially frozen — about 1 1/2 hours.
2. Place the desired ingredient in the center of each cube. Cover the cubes with enough water to approach the top of the tray. Freeze for at least 7 hours or overnight. For best effect, serve in clear cocktails.

Fills one standard 14-cube tray

Variations

● BERRY CUBES: Go with whatever is in season, from raspberries to blueberries, freezing one in each cube. Fun with daiquiris, lemonades, or iced teas.

● CHERRY CUBES: Freeze one whole or half pitted Bing cherry in each cube. For simplicity, use canned cherries.

● CHILI PEPPER CUBES: Freeze a thin slice of dried red pepper or a dice of hot green pepper in each cube for an unexpected kick.

● CITRUS CUBES: Twist a slice of citrus peel into a knot or cut a wedge from a lemon, lime, or blood orange and freeze one in each cube.

● COFFEE CUBES: Substitute strongly brewed coffee for the water. Freeze a chocolate-covered espresso bean in the middle of each cube.

● CUCUMBER CUBES: Freeze a tiny serrated wedge in each cube. Perfect with lemonades, lemon-based cocktails, or drinks made with Pimm's No. 1 liqueur.

● **EDIBLE GOLD LEAF CUBES:** Give holiday or special-occasion cocktails a glamorous shimmer with this amazing paper-thin ingredient, available at most Asian and Indian markets. With scissors, carefully cut the paper into strips measuring 1/8 inch by 1 inch. Place one or more strips in each cube, or place one strip and one tiny edible flower in each cube.

● **FLOWER CUBES:** The perfect touch of class for tropical, tony, or clear cocktails. Try rose petals, pansies, orange blossoms, violets, or other edible flowers. Gently rinse the flowers. Remove any leaves, stems, stamens, or pollen-producing parts. Depending on the size, use the whole flower or just a petal in each cube.

● **FRUIT CUBES:** Freeze a small wedge of pineapple, blood orange, or star fruit in cubes destined for an artistic sangria or a tropical drink.

● **FRUIT JUICE CUBES:** Substitute fruit juice or fruit puree for the water. Add a berry to each cube, if desired.

● **HERB CUBES:** A sprinkle of rosemary, lavender, or thyme leaves in each cube adds a little chic to drinks in need of a subtle something, such as vodka-based cocktails.

● **KUMQUAT CUBES:** These beautiful little orange fruits look smashing floating in ice cubes; use the whole kumquat in the cube, if possible. If it's too big, cut into slices or halves.

● **LIMEADE CUBES:** Combine 3 ounces frozen limeade with 1 can water and fill the tray. Or thoroughly combine 1 1/2 cups water, 2/3 cup fresh lime juice, and 1/3 cup superfine sugar to fill a 20-ounce tray. Freeze 3 to 7 hours.

● **MINT CUBES:** A mint leaf frozen in each cube adds a bright, summery flavor to mint juleps, vodka lemonades, pineapple drinks, or any cocktail that would benefit from a hint of mint.

● **NOVELTY CUBES:** Instead of a standard ice tray, search dime stores and cocktail shops for trays featuring cubes in different shapes, such as stars or hearts. Experiment with adding one or two tiny drops of food coloring to the water for a wild tropical cocktail or offbeat juice drink.

● **SMOOTHIE CUBES:** Replace the water with your favorite bottled smoothie, available refrigerated at many supermarkets and specialty food stores. In a blender, whirl the smoothie cubes with frozen vanilla yogurt and orange juice for a healthy summer shake.

The art of garnishing

Cocktails with a touch of theatrics can set the mood or party theme. Paper umbrellas may be the ultimate retro statement for a tropical drink, but why not plant one in an olive and float it in a martini to take off that serious edge? Unexpected elements, from plastic swordfish to colorful mermaids, add touches of style and humor.

© Matthew Klein/CORBIS

● CITRUS TWISTS (LEMON, LIME, ORANGE) To make the most fragrant twist, use a fresh, unblemished citrus fruit. Organic fruit is best if you can find it. Wash the fruit. Trim off both ends and scoop out the pulp, leaving just the peel. With a sharp paring knife, cut the peel lengthwise into skinny strips or "twists" about 1 1/2 inches long. Or, with a zester or vegetable peeler, pare off a strip of peel, avoiding the bitter white pith just below the peel. Before serving, hold the peel over the glass and twist it clockwise and counterclockwise to squeeze the oil over the surface of the drink. For a more pronounced flavor, drop the twist into the drink.

● CITRUS KNOTS AND OTHER DECORATIVE SHAPES For a different visual approach, follow the directions above but cut the strips 2 to 3 inches long and 1/4 inch wide. Tie the peels into knots, and drop them into the drink. Or cut shapes such as stars, crescent moons, and diamonds out of large sections of the fruit peel. This can be done with a sharp knife or special cocktail cutters. And, if you are having a Martha moment, cut out the letters of your guests' initials to float in their personalized cocktails.

● CITRUS PEEL SPIRALS These add a graceful look to drinks, whether draped over the rim of a cocktail glass or spiraling through tall drinks. With a vegetable peeler or sharp paring knife, make a cut 1/2 inch wide into the peel at one end of the fruit (such as lemon, lime, orange, grapefruit, or blood orange). Pare off a continuous spiral, moving around the fruit.

Coil the peel around your finger, then slowly place it, uncoiling from your finger, into the drink of choice.

● FRUIT WHEELS OR SLICES Consider the endless possibilities when garnishing with fruit, from the traditional citrus wheels to the more festive look of kiwi, star fruit, or blood oranges. To prepare, use a sharp paring knife to trim away the ends of the fruit. Place the fruit on its side and cut crosswise into segments 1/2 inch wide. Make a slit in the center and slide it onto the rim of the glass to garnish.

● SUGARED FRUIT SLICES For an arresting look on a sugar rim, lightly coat a thin slice of orange or lemon or a whole strawberry with superfine sugar. Cut a slit in the middle, and slide the sugared fruit onto the rim to garnish.

Rims and whims

Cocktail art is ripe for revival. We've known the chic of a sugar rim. But in these days of visual wit, kitsch attitudes, and innovation unhinged, how about a Champagne cocktail dressed up with a jeweled turbinado sugar rim, or the tang of a margarita upgraded with a lime-speckled salt rim? Or try a pink coconut rim — the final word from tiki-land. Dip into our collection here, and cut loose with your own fanciful creations.

Rim Basics

1. Chilled glasses are the best vehicle for rims, but an unchilled glass also will work.
2. Pour 5 to 6 tablespoons of the coating ingredient into a small plate or wide, shallow bowl.
3. Depending on the flavor of the drink, rub a lime, lemon, or orange slice around the rim to moisten it. Or, dip the rim in a wide, shallow bowl filled 1/4 inch deep with a fruit juice, grenadine, or a flavored liqueur such as framboise or Cointreau. Choose a flavor to complement or contrast with the cocktail ingredients.
4. Place the rim firmly in the coating ingredients. Gently turn the glass back and forth once to coat, shaking off any excess to form a light or heavy coating, as preferred.
5. Carefully pour the cocktail into the glass, making sure you don't disturb the rim.

Makes enough for 4 rims

Variations

● CHOCOLATE RIMS: A rim of finely grated semisweet chocolate adds just the right edge to cocktails made with coffee or orange liqueurs or lemon flavor. Or try blending equal amounts of finely grated bittersweet chocolate with turbinado sugar.

● CHOCOLATE RIMS WITH ORANGE OR LEMON ZEST: Finely grated semisweet or bittersweet chocolate mixed with a little orange zest can upgrade just about any drink with a chocolate or orange base. For an outrageous Lemon Drop, combine the chocolate with lemon zest.

● CITRUS ZEST RIMS: Citrus is such a basic flavor ingredient to many cocktails, why not draw out its full potential with a citrus zest rim? Mix equal amounts of orange zest and sugar for a cool Cosmopolitan, or mix lemon zest and sugar to rim that bourbon drink or Side Car. Moisten the rim with a complementary juice or liqueur. For a lighter impact, use 1 tablespoon zest to every 2 tablespoons sugar.

● COCOA RIM: Dress up a creamy drink, such as a Brandy Alexander, coconut milk drink, chocolate martini, or a drink featuring coffee-flavored liqueur. Use a lemon to moisten the rim and sweetened cocoa for dipping. Grate a little fresh nutmeg or add about 1 1/2 teaspoons ground nutmeg to the cocoa for a sweet yet pungent perfume.

● COCOA-SUGAR RIM: Moisten the rim with crème de cacao or a complementary juice, such as lime or orange; rim with a blend of unsweetened cocoa powder and superfine sugar.

● COLORED RIMS: This is your opportunity to take advantage of those colored decorator sugar crystals typically used for holiday cookies. Talk about effect! Or combine a small pinch of powdered food coloring with a few tablespoons of sugar; slowly add more color until the desired effect is achieved.

● PINK COCONUT RIM: Moisten the rim of the glass with a complementary liqueur. Mix 3 tablespoons dried unsweetened coconut with 1 tablespoon powdered pink food coloring.

● POWDERED SUGAR RIM: Give tart cocktails such as Side Cars, Lemon Drops, or bourbon drinks a touch of individuality. Moisten with something light, such as fresh lemon. The look should be delicate, so don't overly turn the glass in the sugar.

● SALT AND LIME ZEST RIM: This, plus a rocking margarita, equals icy bliss. Use equal proportions of kosher salt and lime zest.

● SALT RIM: Moisten the rim with a lemon or lime wedge. Coarse kosher salt will produce the best texture. For a wilder look, try colored specialty salts found at supermarkets.

● SALT AND SUGAR RIM: For margaritas or blended fruit drinks, this combo adds a whole level of intrigue. Moisten the rim with a lime. Combine equal amounts of kosher salt and granulated sugar. For a more dramatic effect, use sparkling turbinado sugar.

● SUGAR RIM: Use anything from a citrus wedge to your favorite liqueur to moisten the rim; for the sugar, a superfine grade is best.

● TURBINADO SUGAR RIM: Try turbinado sugar in place of granulated sugar for a chunky, amber-hued rim with its own rock crystal glow.

● VANILLA SUGAR RIM: To add a sensuous vanilla scent to a sugar rim, place a whole vanilla bean in a jar of sugar, cover with an airtight lid, and let sit for 2 weeks at room temperature. A commercial version is available at specialty stores.

Syrups and sours

Fresh sweet-and-sour mix and homemade syrups — built around fruits, spices, or herbs and used in place of sugar — add quality and innovation to the cocktail arts. By some quirk of science, it seems impossible to duplicate a drink exactly, no matter how carefully you pour. But you can have a terrific one every time if you invest in the best ingredients you can afford and learn a few easy recipes that celebrate flavor and flair.

Syrups

● SUGAR SYRUP

This is also known as "simple syrup" and for good reason — if you can combine sugar and water and turn on a burner, you're there. But why bother when sugar is just a teaspoon away? Because sugar syrup dissolves and blends beautifully, while granulated sugar can make a drink grainy. The formula below can be multiplied or cut in half. When refrigerated, the syrup will keep up to 1 month. While fresh is definitely best, we won't tell if you buy bottled sugar syrup at your local liquor store.

- ● $1/2$ cup water
- ● 1 cup sugar

1. In a small saucepan, bring the water to a boil. Remove the pan from the heat and add the sugar. Stir until the sugar is completely dissolved.

2. Cool completely. Pour into a clean glass jar and cap tightly. Store in the refrigerator and use as needed.

Makes 1 cup

● GINGER SYRUP

This spicy sugar syrup brings an exotic tone to iced teas, fruit drinks, and citrus-based cocktails — or combine with sparkling water for a zippy ginger ale. When refrigerated, the syrup will keep up to 2 weeks.

- ● 1 cup water
- ● $1/2$ cup sliced fresh ginger
- ● 1 cup sugar

1. In a small saucepan, bring the water to a boil. Lower the heat and stir in the ginger. Cover and remove the pan from the heat. Let stand for 1 hour or until the desired flavor intensity is reached.

2. Strain the mixture into another saucepan. Bring the ginger water to a boil over medium-high heat. Remove the pan from the heat and add the sugar. Stir until the sugar is completely dissolved.

3. Cool completely. Pour into a clean glass jar and cap tightly. Store in the refrigerator and use as needed.

Makes $1 1/2$ cups

Variations

● **CINNAMON SYRUP:**
Replace the ginger with 1
tablespoon ground cinnamon.

● **CLOVE SYRUP:** Replace the
ginger with 1 tablespoon
ground cloves.

● **LEMON OR LIME SYRUP:**
Replace the ginger with $1/2$ cup
lemon or lime zest.

● **MINT OR BASIL SYRUP:**
Replace the ginger with $1/2$ cup
fresh mint or basil leaves.

● **ORANGE SYRUP:** Replace
the ginger with $1/2$ cup orange
zest.

● **TEA SYRUP:** Replace the
water with strongly steeped tea
(from black to green, Earl Grey
to Red Zinger). Eliminate the
ginger and increase the sugar
to 2 cups.

● **VANILLA SYRUP:** Replace
the ginger with 1 vanilla bean.

Sweet and Sour

Sure, you can grab the
premade mix at the store. But
nothing compares to your own
balance of light and sharp,
sweet and tart. For the best
flavor, use filtered or spring
water instead of tap water.
When refrigerated in a clean,
covered jar, the mix will keep
up to 10 days.

● $1/4$ cup sugar syrup (see
facing page)
● $3/4$ cup fresh lime juice

● $3/4$ cup fresh squeezed
lemon juice
● $1/4$ cup water

1. Pour all the ingredients
into a clean 20-ounce glass
container with an airtight lid.

2. Twist on the lid and shake
the contents together until well
mixed.

3. Refrigerate until needed.

Makes 2 cups

Infusion fusion

Turn plain vodka into a sparkplug for fanciful cocktails or play with exotic fruits and rum for sumptuous daiquiris, punches, and tropical drinks. Infused liquors are delicious on their own and handy for giving drinks an instant flash of depth and complexity.

Basic infusion guidelines

1. Use a clean, large glass container (at least 1.5 liters) with an airtight lid.
2. Start with 1 liter good-quality vodka, rum, tequila, or other versatile base ingredient. Empty the liter into the glass container and save the bottle for bottling the final infusion.
3. Add fresh ripe fruit, herbs, spices, or even vegetables such as cucumbers. Close tightly, swirl gently to combine the ingredients, and let stand at room temperature. Infusion times vary, depending on the ingredients. Strong flavors such as lemon or rosemary may need only 24 to 48 hours; milder flavors such as raspberries may take 1 to 3 weeks to fully infuse. To get the desired flavor, taste frequently and gently swirl the contents every few days.
4. If the ingredients break down and the liquid is cloudy, strain the mixture slowly through a cheesecloth-lined wire strainer.

● BERRY OR FRUIT VODKA
Fruity or citrus-based cocktails, such as the Cosmopolitan, reach their pinnacle with flavored homemade vodka. Raspberry vodka is one of the most popular flavors.

• 1 liter good-quality vodka
• 3 cups fresh, rinsed berries or fresh pineapple, mango, or seeded watermelon, peeled and sliced

1. Pour the bottle of vodka into a 1.5-liter glass container with an airtight lid. Add the berries or fruit; swirl the contents to combine. Twist on the lid.

2. Infuse at room temperature for 1 to 3 weeks, swirling the contents and tasting for the desired flavor intensity level every few days.

3. When ready, using a large, fine-mesh wire strainer and a funnel, strain the infused mixture back into the original vodka bottle. Cap tightly and refrigerate until serving.

Makes 1 liter

Variations
CITRUS VODKA: Follow directions for Berry or Fruit Vodka, above, substituting the peel of a

large lemon, orange, tangerine, or lime for the berries or fruit. Let stand for 24 to 48 hours.

COFFEE BEAN VODKA:
Follow directions for Berry or Fruit Vodka, substituting 20 coffee beans for the berries or fruit. Let stand for 24 to 48 hours.

HERB OR SPICE VODKA:
Follow directions for Berry or Fruit Vodka, substituting 2 cups fresh mint leaves, 1/2 cup of fresh rosemary, or 25 whole cloves for the berries or fruit. Let stand for 24 to 48 hours.

VANILLA VODKA: Follow directions for Berry or Fruit Vodka, substituting 2 vanilla beans for the berries or fruit. Let stand for 24 to 48 hours.

● **PINEAPPLE-INFUSED RUM**
Infused rums are the ticket to an instant tropical adventure.

● 1 whole fresh pineapple
● 1 liter good-quality light rum

1. Peel and core the pineapple. Dice the fruit into 1/4-inch pieces.
2. Pour the rum into a 1.5-liter glass container with an air-

tight lid. Add the pineapple, gently swirl to combine the ingredients, and twist on the lid. Infuse at room temperature for 2 weeks, swirling the contents and tasting for the desired flavor intensity every few days. Steep another week for stronger flavor.

3. When ready, using a large, fine-mesh wire strainer and a funnel, strain the infused mixture back into the original rum bottle. Cap tightly and refrigerate until serving.

Makes 1 liter

● **COCONUT-INFUSED RUM**
Consider this the perfect quaff to accompany Asian or Indonesian feasts, or the transforming ingredient in a beach cocktail.

● 1 liter good-quality light rum
● 3 cups unsweetened coconut, freshly grated or store-bought
● 1 small piece of vanilla bean

1. Pour the rum into a 1.5-liter glass container with an airtight lid. Add the coconut and vanilla bean and twist on the lid. Infuse at room temperature for 3 weeks, swirling

gently and tasting for the desired flavor intensity every 3 to 4 days.

2. When ready, using a large, fine-mesh wire strainer and a funnel, strain the infused mixture back into the original rum bottle. Cap tightly and refrigerate until serving.

Makes 1 liter

Chapter 1

high heel seductions

First of all, you want The Look.
Maybe it's a flirty chiffon dress
or a sexy bustier under a
weathered fly-boy jacket —
or even that screen-siren
dress with the naughty
neckline. So far, so good.
But if you really want to
rev up for a night to remember, it's all about perfect
cocktails and killer heels.

- **Gin and sin**
- **Spy girl**
- **Getting layered**
- **Blonde bombshell**
- **Stiletto cocktail**
- **Silk stockings**
- **Hot lips**

From ankle-rockin' slingbacks to seductive T-strap sandals, elevation is the object. So walk tall, tailor the drink to the trap, and don't forget to leave a lipstick print on the rim — the ultimate message in a glass. From women of mystery to wives in search of the Tiffany's box, these liquid temptations will make a night last forever.

Gin and sin

The beauty of gin is the way it evokes that husky, gravel voice, a sound at once vulnerable and take-charge. All traces of shy, retiring, wilting violet vanish in the citrus bite of a drink that's been around since women wore pillbox hats, pedal-pushers, and patent-leather pumps. Don't mess with the formula — it's had more than 50 years of road-testing and is geared to provoke the trouble you're looking for.

- 6 ice cubes
- 4 ounces gin
- 2 teaspoons fresh lemon juice
- 2 teaspoons fresh orange juice
- 2 to 4 dashes grenadine

1. Fill a cocktail shaker with the ice and pour in the remaining ingredients. Stir very gently with a long-handled bar spoon to chill, about 20 revolutions.

2. Strain the mixture, and divide between two short old-fashioned glasses.

Serves 2

Spy girl

Say you're one of those espionage types, equally adept at weaving and darting elegantly through a Neiman Marcus sale and snooping around your boyfriend's e-mail. You've got a black belt in seduction, can rotate tires, and play a steel hand of poker. Your drink of choice is tart and sassy — and, of course, shaken not stirred. Consider this your own special spy-girl combo: intriguing, well-traveled, and adventurous right down to the bittersweet shadows of Italian Campari.

- 1 1/2 cups cracked ice or 6 ice cubes
- 1/4 cup grapefruit juice
- 2 ounces top-quality gin, such as Bombay Sapphire
- 2 ounces Lillet Blanc
- 2 splashes Campari
- 2 splashes sweet vermouth

GARNISH
- 2 spiraling grapefruit peels (see page 15)

1. Chill two 6-ounce martini glasses.

2. Fill a cocktail shaker with the ice and add all the ingredients except the garnish. Shake vigorously to blend and chill.

3. Strain the mixture evenly between the glasses. Drape one grapefruit spiral over each rim to garnish.

Serves 2

Getting layered

What could be a better come-on than "Wanna get layered?" But the *real* fun is watching your date's expression when you return to the living room with liqueurs instead of lacy lingerie. Your mission: create a pousse-café, a multileveled drink worth making just to whisper the words, *poos ka-FAY*. As you pour, each ingredient lays on top of the next, creating its own color stratum and taste temptation. The choice of flavor partners is wide open, as long as each addition is lighter in weight. The following combination is, no doubt, a favorite of Masters & Johnson, and possibly Dr. Ruth. The perfect outfit for the occasion? Sheer hostess pajamas and spring-o-later shoes, of course.

- 2 ounces Cognac
- 1 ounce apricot brandy
- 1/2 ounce sweet cream

1. Divide the Cognac between two shot glasses or pousse-café glasses.

2. To create the next layer, invert a teaspoon over one of the glasses, tip-end angled slightly down and just touching the side of the glass. Slowly pour half of the apricot brandy over the back of the spoon so that it floats on top of the Cognac. Repeat the process with the remaining apricot brandy in the other glass.

3. Float half of the cream on top of each drink to serve.

Serves 2

Blonde bombshell

Like all notorious blondes, this one looks rather harmless and unassuming. But the deeper you go, the more hooked you get on a comely drink that pulses with pear, hazelnut, and cream. Remember: There's a Marilyn in every girl. Whisper softly, sip demurely, and purr like a kitten. Just resist that urge to sing "Happy Birthday, Mr. President."

- 1 1/2 cups crushed ice or 6 ice cubes
- 3 ounces pear nectar or juice
- 3 ounces pear brandy
- 2 tablespoons Frangelico (hazelnut liqueur)
- 2 ounces half-and-half

GARNISH
- 2 thin pear slices
- 2 pinches cinnamon

1. Chill two 6-ounce cocktail glasses.

2. Fill a cocktail shaker with the ice. Add the remaining ingredients except the garnishes. Shake vigorously to blend and chill.

3. Strain the mixture evenly between the chilled glasses.

4. Cut a deep slit in the center of each pear slice and place one on each rim. Finish the drinks with a pinch of cinnamon on top.

Serves 2

VARIATION Prepare each glass with a sugar rim (see page 17) and substitute Amaretto for the Frangelico.

Stiletto cocktail

So, you think a woman's drink is some froufrou frappé sweet enough to melt your molars? Well, sure, if you're talking about Gidget bar-hopping in Honolulu. But this classic '50s combo is for another kind of gal altogether: elusive, magnetic, a no-nonsense woman who invites her guest inside for a late-night bourbon and razor-sharp repartee. You won't need to pop in a film noir video in the VCR for atmosphere — you're it, baby. Power, culture, femininity, and a hint of danger — all in a glass. Just remember, when you walk across his chest with those spike heels, show no mercy.

- 1½ cups cracked ice
- 6 ounces Amaretto
- 3 ounces good Kentucky bourbon
- 2 ounces fresh lemon juice
- 2 tablespoons sugar syrup (see page 18)
- 10 or 12 ice cubes

GARNISH
- 2 lemon peels

1. Fill a cocktail shaker with the cracked ice and add the Amaretto, bourbon, lemon juice, and sugar syrup. Shake vigorously to blend and chill.

2. Divide the ice cubes between two old-fashioned glasses. Strain half the mixture into each glass.

3. To garnish, use one lemon twist per glass. Twist a peel over the top of each drink. Rub the peel around the rim of the glass, then drop it into the drink to serve.

Serves 2

Silk stockings

Mingling creamy sophistication with a tease of chocolate, this pale pink number is everything a silk stocking should be: very smooth, very sexy, totally irresistible.

- 3 ounces gold tequila
- 3 ounces white crème de cacao
- 3 ounces half-and-half
- 2 splashes of grenadine
- 1 cup crushed ice
- Ground cinnamon for dusting

1. Chill two 6-ounce martini glasses.

2. In a blender combine the tequila, crème de cacao, half-and-half, grenadine, and crushed ice. Blend until frothy, chilled, and well combined.

3. Divide the mixture evenly between the two chilled glasses. Dust a little ground cinnamon on top and serve.

Serves 2

Finally a sullen gate over the ba...
and all the [illegible] boked...
[illegible] cafe—from having done if...
out of every now and tramp in [illegible]...

So Derrick I mark...
delight.

Yours,

"Hot Lips"

CANNES

Hot lips

You've talked the fire down to coals. Now what? Think fast. How can you up the romance amps without blowing the fuse? Move the action to the kitchen, light some candles, and get the radio tuned to the mood. Then heat up this steamy tonic of malt and almond hues, perfect for sipping between slow-dance moves in front of the microwave. Guaranteed to cross your wires.

- 1 tablespoon toasted almond cream liqueur
- 1 ounce Amaretto
- 1 1/2 cups milk
- 1 tablespoon malted milk powder
- Pinch of ground coriander

1. Divide the toasted almond cream liqueur and Amaretto between two Irish coffee glasses or heatproof mugs.

2. Warm the milk in a saucepan over medium heat, whisking vigorously with a wire whisk until hot and frothy, about 1 minute. (Or steam the milk in an espresso machine.)

3. Pour a little hot milk into each glass. Divide the malted milk powder between the glasses and whisk briskly with a fork to combine. Divide the remaining milk evenly between the two glasses, spooning any foam over the top.

4. Serve hot with a pinch of coriander on top.

Serves 2

VARIATION Add 1 to 2 tablespoons espresso to the milk.

Chapter 2

mad about margaritas

Nobody has a problem recognizing the quintessential guy drink: straight up or on the rocks, gloom in a glass, or hail-thee-well, dude! No frills, no fuss, no changing the game plan. Trying to define the perfect girl drink is more challenging. It must be multifaceted, playful, daring, and visually appealing, with no limits on the fun factor. In a word, margarita. We've created a version for just about every mood known to the female soul: the perfectionist who must nail the classic, the adventuress, the hostess, and the temptress, not to mention the creative hedonist for whom a chocolate margarita makes perfect sense. The tequila market has come of age, and the key to a killer margarita is finding a brand labeled 100 percent agave and reposado, sure signs of quality. Think silver for fruity or spicy versions, gold for warmer tones.

- **Margarita's ultimate margarita**

- **Strawberry-guavaritas**

- **Choco locos**

- **Venus envy**

- **Creamsicle margarita**

- **Fallen angelita**

Margarita's ultimate margarita

Here it is: margarita ground zero, lab-tested and hot-wired for flavor. What separates this version is a sublime golden shimmer, courtesy of saffron threads and the inventiveness of Portland artist Margarita Leon. For a beautiful orchid garnish, buy a stem of Dendrobium orchids, blossomed with 6 to 10 tiny, nonedible flowers.

- Salt rim (see page 17)
- 1 scant tablespoon sugar
- 1 1/4 tablespoons fresh lime juice
- 1 pinch saffron threads
- 1 1/2 cups crushed ice
- 1 1/2 ounces premium silver tequila
- 1/2 ounce Triple Sec
- 4 to 6 ice cubes

GARNISH
- 1 lime twist
- 1 baby orchid

1. Chill a margarita glass or an 8-ounce cocktail glass. Salt the rim and return the glass to the freezer.

2. Combine the sugar and lime juice in a small bowl. Add the saffron, crushing the threads between your fingers. Stir until the sugar dissolves and the mixture is somewhat syrupy.

3. Fill a cocktail shaker with the crushed ice. Add the tequila, Triple Sec, and the sugar-lime mixture. Shake vigorously to blend and chill.

4. Fill the prepared glass with the ice cubes. Strain the shaken mixture into the glass. Twist the lime twist over the top, then drop it into the drink. Spear the bottom of the orchid with an elongated cocktail pick, and balance it on the rim to garnish.

Serves 1

Strawberry-guavaritas

A couple of these and you can forget the French paradox, chaos theory, and Pascal's unsolvable math problem. Let's concentrate instead on why we cut our bangs to make them grow. There's no end to what you might ponder when a strawberry margarita frolics with guava nectar and enough black raspberry liqueur to wet the lips with a juicy pink stain.

- 1 1/2 ounces silver tequila
- 3/4 ounce Cointreau
- 1 1/2 ounces Sweet and Sour (see page 19)
- 2 ounces guava nectar or juice
- 1/4 ounce Chambord
- 1/2 to 3/4 cup sliced strawberries
- 1 1/2 cups cracked ice

GARNISH
- 2 lime wedges
- 4 strawberries or raspberries

1. In a blender, whirl the tequila, Cointreau, Sweet and Sour, guava nectar, and Chambord for a few seconds, just enough to combine. Add the sliced strawberries and ice. Blend until slushy, frothy, and chilled.

2. Divide the mixture evenly between two margarita glasses or large wine goblets.

3. With a plastic toothpick sword, skewer a lime wedge between two of the berries and pop into the drink; repeat the process to garnish the remaining drink.

Serves 2

Choco locos

Decadent, divine, okay . . . disgraceful. But then again, chocolate is always in season and best appreciated by anybody born with a double-X chromosome, estrogen-laced DNA, and a craving for shoes. This is possibly the world's first chocolate margarita, *muy elegante*, we might add. More tart than sweet, it glistens with a topaz afterglow brought on by Godiva liqueur, known for its serious chocolate buzz.

- Turbinado sugar rim (optional, see page 17)
- 1 1/2 cups cracked ice
- 1 1/2 ounces good-quality gold tequila
- 3/4 ounce Cointreau
- 1 1/2 ounces Godiva liqueur
- 1 1/2 ounces Sweet and Sour (see page 19)
- 1/2 ounce fresh orange juice

GARNISH
- 2 orange twists
- Mexican chocolate shavings

1. Sugar the rim of two 6-ounce cocktail glasses if desired. Chill the glasses.

2. Fill a cocktail shaker with the ice. Add all the ingredients except the garnishes. Shake vigorously to blend and chill.

3. Strain the mixture evenly between the prepared glasses.

4. Twist an orange twist over the top of one glass, then drop it into the drink. Shave a little Mexican chocolate over the top. Repeat the process with the second drink.

Serves 2

Venus envy

You haven't heard of it, but neither had the Barefoot Contessa. Yet Damiana Liqueur, the legendary herbal aphrodisiac, should be enshrined in your medicine cabinet. Forget oysters, ginseng, and other fire starters. Made from a Mexican mountain plant, Damiana transforms tequila and lime into something as silky as a camisole, as hypnotic as hot sand. Wildly popular in Baja, this flowery potion is now bewitching America, where it is often called "liqueur for lovers."

- 1 1/2 cups cracked ice or 6 ice cubes
- 2 1/2 ounces good-quality gold tequila
- 1 1/2 ounces Damiana Liqueur
- 3 ounces Sweet and Sour (see page 19)

1. Chill two 6-ounce martini glasses.

2. Fill a cocktail shaker with the ice and add the tequila, Damiana, and Sweet and Sour. Shake vigorously to blend and chill.

3. Strain the mixture evenly between the chilled glasses.

Serves 2

Creamsicle margarita

This is a light, creamy departure from the traditional margarita. Here orange sorbet and Tuaca liqueur play beautifully against the swaggering beat of warm tequila. Think the Good Humor Man meets *I Love Lucy*. More than two of these and you'll have some splainin' to do.

- Sugar rim (see page 17)
- 1 1/2 ounces good-quality gold tequila
- 3/4 ounce Tuaca liqueur
- 1 1/2 ounces Sweet and Sour (see page 19)
- 1 ounce fresh orange juice
- 1 ounce half-and-half
- 1/2 cup orange sorbet
- 1 1/2 cups crushed ice

GARNISH
- 2 orange slices

1. Sugar the rims of two margarita or large cocktail glasses. Chill the glasses.

2. In a blender, whirl the tequila, Tuaca, Sweet and Sour, orange juice, and half-and-half for a few seconds, just enough to combine. Add the orange sorbet and ice. Blend until thick, slushy, frothy, and chilled.

3. Divide the mixture evenly between the prepared glasses. Cut a deep slit in the center of each orange slice. Slide a slice onto each rim to garnish.

Serves 2

Fallen angelita

Girlfriends, it's time to combine a little New Age therapy with your minimum nightly requirements: tequila, sugar, salt, and loose lips. Sure, we can bless the beasts and the children, but for one evening, can't we be totally self-absorbed? Forget the tortured fat-free quesadillas — rip into bags of chocolate chip cookies, munch on nuevo chips, and experiment with dips. Through it all, sip a margarita sharpened with hazelnut liqueur and the crackle of cranberry.

- Salt rim (see page 17)
- 1 1/2 cups crushed ice
- 3 ounces good-quality gold tequila
- 2 ounces Grand Marnier
- 3 ounces Sweet and Sour (see page 19)
- 1 ounce cranberry juice
- 1/2 ounce Frangelico

GARNISH
- 1 lime slice
- 2 cranberries

1. Salt the rim of a margarita glass or a 10-ounce wine goblet, then chill the glass.

2. Fill a shaker with the ice and add all the ingredients except the garnish. Shake vigorously to blend and chill.

3. Strain the mixture into the prepared glass. With a plastic sword toothpick, skewer the lime slice between the cranberries and pop into the drink to serve.

Serves 1

Chapter 3

altered states

This collection of mood balloons is in a sky of its own. It's meant for those special moments when irrational thinking is trip-wired by mysterious internal battle zones, the humidity level, and the possibility of life after the phone call that never happened. Sit back, sip one of these wild cards, put it all into perspective, and remember: there's nothing a pair of new shoes and a trip to the lipstick counter won't fix.

- **Shirley Temple's evil twin**
- **Bad hair day blaster**
- **Minivan mom meltdown mixer**
- **Rx for pms**
- **Chocolate-mint hormone replacement therapy**

Shirley Temple's evil twin

Good-bye Little Missy. Farewell, Good Ship Lollipop. No more "Oh, thank you, gee whiz, Mr. So-and-So." The bubbly-pink soda sipped by a million 10-year-old princesses since the '50s has grown up and become a lot more interesting. Say hello to a whole new steel-toed tap dance: a drink with a mischievous kick, right down to the vampy black cherry cubes. One of these and you'll want to throw Leo overboard for Tony Soprano. And you can salute to that.

- 6 cherry ice cubes (see page 13)
- 1 1/2 ounces Kirschwasser or cherry brandy
- Splash of grenadine
- 4 to 5 ounces 7-Up or ginger ale

1. Chill a 10-ounce glass.

2. Fill the chilled glass with the cherry ice cubes. Add the Kirschwassers or cherry brandy and the grenadine.

3. Top with the 7-Up or ginger ale and serve with a long straw.

Serves 1

Bad hair day blaster

It's one of those days when you're thinking Julia Roberts but your mirror suggests that dishing up meat loaf would be a good career move if a hair net came with the uniform. Our advice: scuttle the herbal-infused head wrap, the Peruvian organic verbena mayonnaise, the egg white smear, and the vanilla latté mousse. Sometimes bad hair happens to good people. On these occasions, indulge in a drink that tastes like a chocolate chip cookie. It's better than blowing a paycheck on a stress-melting shiatsu scalp massage, not to mention a good excuse for blowing off a day of work.

- ¹/₂ ounce chocolate almond liqueur, chilled
- ¹/₂ ounce dark crème de cacao
- ¹/₂ ounce chilled Baileys Irish Cream

1. Pour the chocolate almond liqueur into a chilled shot glass.

2. Invert a teaspoon over the shot glass, tip-end angled slightly down and just touching the side of the glass. Slowly pour the dark crème de cacao over the back of the spoon so that it floats on top of the chocolate almond liqueur.

3. Repeat the process with the Baileys Irish Cream to finish the drink.

Serves 1

Minivan mom meltdown mixer

When too many soccer practice shuttles collide with a relentlessly cheerful boy-band CD set permanently on instant replay; when your neurons bristle from the back-seat accretions of petrified French fries; when your expression increasingly resembles Edvard Munch's *The Scream*, it's time to head for home. Set your brain on idle, flop in a tub with anti-inner frenzy herbs dredged up from some Tibetan canyon, then coast with this light, cucumber-lemon cocktail. Believe us, you'll be ready to log another 100 miles again tomorrow.

- 5 thin cucumber slices
- 5 ice cubes
- 1 ounce well-chilled vodka
- 1 1/2 ounces Pimm's No. 1
- 4 ounces lemonade

GARNISH
- 1 lemon wedge
- Two 1/4-inch-thick cucumber slices

1. Place one of the thin cucumber slices in the bottom of a highball glass. Top with one of the ice cubes. Add the remaining thin cucumber slices and ice cubes in alternating layers, ending with an ice cube on top.

2. Pour in the vodka, Pimm's No.1, and lemonade. Stir with a long-handled bar spoon to chill and combine.

3. With a plastic sword toothpick, skewer the lemon wedge between the two 1/4- inch-thick cucumber slices; pop into the drink to serve.

Serves 1

SS-COUNTRY
DER SPREE

7
TCHES
OF
ATH

HUSETTS

NDIT
O
RED
LF

INDIANA

AN URGE CAME
ON ME TO KILL

$\mathcal{R}$x for pms

You're feeling puffy, bloated, and fat (so what else is new?). Yesterday you were a cool chick. Today you're an edgy, hormone-surging stress machine stalking chocolate counters and ready to mind-shred your sweet boyfriend into a simpering bowl of oatmeal. The urge for an impulse buy is building. Before you drop $400 on that rhinestone cowgirl outfit, we've concocted an antidote for irrational thoughts: the flavors of honey-whiskey (sweet comes with bitter), black vodka (stop worrying and learn to love the gloom factor), and cream (remember, white clouds always follow stormy days). Knock this back, take two chocolate truffles, and don't call *anyone* in the morning.

- 1 ounce Drambuie
- 1/2 ounce chilled black vodka
- 1/4 ounce chilled sweet cream

1. In a large chilled shot glass, combine the Drambuie and black vodka.

2. Slowly float the sweet cream on top to serve.

Serves 1

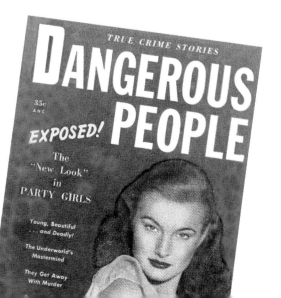

TRUE CRIME STORIES

DANGEROUS PEOPLE

35¢
ANC

EXPOSED!

The "New Look" in PARTY GIRLS

Young, Beautiful . . . and Deadly!

The Underworld's Mastermind

They Get Away With Murder

Chocolate-mint hormone replacement therapy

Call it a midlife cocktail — a treatment to defy your endocrinologist when taken orally at critical moments, like when it seems normal to park your head in the freezer, pack yourself in dry ice, wipe your brow with a squeegee, or ship yourself UPS to an estrogen factory. This taste sensation is so cooling, so completely self-indulgent and divinely inspired, you may want to start having hot flashes on purpose. Serve with hand-held fans and tissues.

- 2 Oreo cookies, broken into pieces
- 1 1/2 ounces Cognac
- 1 1/2 ounces Godiva liqueur
- 5 fresh mint leaves (no stems)
- 1 cup chocolate-mint ice cream
- 1/2 cup crushed ice

GARNISH
- 1 mint sprig

1. Pulverize the Oreo cookies in a blender until reduced to fine crumbs. Add the Cognac, Godiva liqueur, and mint leaves. Blend until frothy — it's okay if the mixture is textured with mint and cookie crumbs. Add the chocolate-mint ice cream and crushed ice. Blend until thick and smooth.

2. Pour into a large wine goblet and garnish with the mint sprig.

Serves 1

Chapter 4

new girl classics

Forget about grasshoppers, Brandy Alexanders, and all those caloric explosions aimed at females of the '50s. Not that we're against sweet drinks . . . but we like them with complexity, lots of flavor nuances, swank rims, and inventive garnishes. And we're not afraid of drinks with a bite. On the other hand, liquor that tastes like a root beer float does sound pretty swell. So who said we're not full of contradictions?

- **That cosmo girl**
- **Lemon drop**
- **Colette's car**
- **Root beer float**
- **Debutonics**
- **Midori sour**

That cosmo girl

The Cosmopolitan remains the "It Girl" drink. Perfect for any occasion, it's chic but unpretentious, and equally appropriate for hip hostessing; sexy, late-night sipping; or two friends coping with shopper's remorse. Fresh lime and cranberry juice are prerequisites for entering the real-deal tart zone. But our version goes into hyperspace with its own galaxy of floating garnishes.

- 1 1/2 cups cracked ice or 6 ice cubes
- 1 1/2 ounces citron or raspberry vodka
- 1/2 ounce fresh lime juice
- 1/2 ounce Triple Sec
- 1 ounce cranberry juice

GARNISH
- One 1/2-inch piece orange peel, cut into a star shape
- One 1/2-inch piece lemon peel, cut into a crescent moon shape
- One 1/2-inch piece lime peel, cut into a round planet shape

1. Chill a 6-ounce cocktail glass.

2. Fill a cocktail shaker with the ice and add the citron or raspberry vodka, lime juice, Triple Sec, and cranberry juice. Shake vigorously to blend and chill.

3. Strain the mixture into the chilled glass.

4. Float the star, moon, and planet shapes on top to garnish.

Serves 1

Lemon drop

It started with a lemonade stand on the sidewalk next to your parents' drive-way, when you made $1.15 on a blistering July afternoon. That sweet, light, always-on-the-edge flavor of youth has grown up and become a force of cock-tail culture, with its irresistible snap and slick sugar rim. Our secret is the slight, almost imperceptible beat of fresh orange juice, which brings up the lemon flavor while adding a mysterious luster.

- Sugar rim (see page 17)
- 1 1/2 cups cracked ice or 6 ice cubes
- 1 1/2 ounces lemon vodka
- 2 ounces fresh lemon juice
- 1 ounce fresh orange juice
- 1 1/2 to 3 teaspoons superfine sugar

GARNISH
- 1 lemon spiral (see page 15)

1. Sugar the rim of a 6-ounce cocktail glass, and chill the glass.

2. Fill a cocktail shaker with the ice and add the vodka, lemon juice, orange juice, and sugar. Shake vigorously to blend and chill; taste and adjust for sweetness.

3. Strain the mixture into the prepared glass and garnish with the lemon spiral.

Serves 1

Colette's car

Portland cocktail philosopher Michael Autrey has a theory on how drinks are created: "Customers become crabby and bartenders become innovative." So one night, when a woman demanded "a Side Car that isn't really a Side Car," he turbo-charged the standard brandy-orange-lime combo with Armagnac, a nutty, Cognac-like French brandy, and *Punt e Mes*, a bittersweet vermouth with its own spice aura. The apricot-colored results, full of big fruity flavors and toasty aromas, could rev up any palate. Hop in and drive, baby.

- 6 ice cubes
- 3 to 4 ounces fresh orange, blood orange, or tangerine juice
- 3/4 to 1 ounce fresh lime juice
- 1/2 ounce Grand Marnier
- 1/2 to 3/4 ounce *Punt e Mes*
- 3 ounces Armagnac
- 2 splashes sugar syrup (optional, see page 18)

1. Chill a 10-ounce martini glass or large wine goblet.

2. Fill a cocktail shaker with the ice cubes. Add all the ingredients, except the sugar syrup. Shake vigorously to blend and chill. Sweeten with sugar syrup if desired.

3. Strain the mixture into the chilled glass and serve.

Serves 1

Root beer float

This is dessert in a glass, divinity upon demand, regression without having to analyze the Freudian implications of it all. How come we never got these at summer camp? The root beer taste comes from Galliano, a sweet, anise-tinged liqueur. If you're really cutting loose, spoon a little whipped cream on top, and count the calories tomorrow (or better, don't count them at all). This formula comes from Higgins, a hip Oregon restaurant, where innovative bartender Nancy Cheek finds it a hit with female customers.

- 6 to 8 ice cubes
- 1 1/4 ounces Kahlua or other coffee liqueur
- 1/2 ounce vodka
- Splash of cola
- 4 ounces half-and-half
- 1/4 ounce Galliano

GARNISH
- 1 maraschino cherry

1. Fill a 12-ounce chimney glass with the ice cubes.

2. Slowly pour in the Kahlua, vodka, splash of cola, half-and-half, and Galliano. Do not stir, but rather let each ingredient settle into its own layer.

3. Top off with the maraschino cherry to serve.

Serves 1

Debutonics

If you never got your shot at the coming-out party, this is it. Drag out that prom gown, the elbow-length white gloves, the falsies, and the Cadillac-pink lipstick. Our suggestion for this occasion: no boys, no two-drink minimum, no back stabbing, no fake smiles. Serve finger sandwiches, fussy pastries, and our special gin and tonic, glistening with lime ice cubes and the essential Euro-tones of Campari. Proportions multiply easily for a crowd. Oh, and congratulations — you've arrived.

- 4 to 5 limeade ice cubes (see page 14)
- 1 1/2 ounces good-quality gin
- Splash of Campari
- 3 to 4 ounces tonic water

GARNISH
- 1 lime wedge

1. Chill an 8-ounce double old-fashioned glass.

2. Fill the chilled glass with the ice cubes. Add the gin and splash of Campari. Top with the tonic.

3. Squeeze the lime wedge over the top, then drop it into the drink to garnish.

Serves 1

Midori sour

When cocktails became a required player in the suave nightclub scene of the '50s, sours inspired their own history, especially among women. The basic notes are always the same: loud citrus sounds mellowed by sweet tones and a liquor that can power the rhythm. This number is amplified by an electric chartreuse color and a super sour tang with just enough sugar to take the edge off. Midori liqueur, with its intense jolt of melon flavor, has given sours a whole new audience.

- Powdered sugar rim (see page 17)
- 1 cup cracked ice or 6 ice cubes
- 2 ounces Midori liqueur
- 1 ounce lime juice
- 1 ounce lemon juice
- 1 tablespoon superfine sugar

GARNISH
- 2 honeydew melon balls (optional)

1. Sugar the rim of a 6-ounce cocktail glass, then chill the glass.

2. Fill a cocktail shaker with the ice. Add the Midori, lime juice, lemon juice, and sugar.

3. Shake vigorously to blend and chill. Strain the mixture into the prepared glass.

4. With a plastic sword toothpick, skewer the melon balls and balance the pick on the rim of the glass to garnish.

Serves 1

Chapter 5

sol sisters

If girls have a season all their own, it's summer. Bring on the days of cocoa butter and cool shades; tank tops and cheating with insta-tan; steamy romances and 3 A.M. mood walks; ice cream in the freezer and ice cubes in every drink. Summer is so full of expressions — from lush to blithe, impulsive to all-out vegetative — every notion requires its own special mix. The following selections are on-call for fear-of-swimsuit parties, post-convertible beach jaunts, heat defiance, tropical fantasies, and spontaneous culinary shindigs — from patio brunches to backyard barbecues.

- **Bikinitini**

- **Brazilian sugarcane coffee shake**

- **Pineapple coconut zowee**

- **Hot as Haiti**

- **Pink melon fever**

- **Surfer girl**

Bikinitini

As far as drinks go, this is practically a vitamin — apply directly to the thighs for a slim new you, or serve as a lean party drink (save those extra cucumber sticks for morning-after, under-eye therapy). This crisp, sea-green elixir is *the* perfect poolside drink — dibs on the diving board!!! Pour a round, then get the coven together for a special burning of the *Sports Illustrated* swimsuit issue.

GARNISH
- 1 small cucumber, for cucumber sticks

- 4 ounces vodka
- 2 ounces Triple Sec
- 2 ounces fresh lemon juice
- 1 cup peeled, seeded, and cubed cucumber
- 4 fresh mint leaves (optional)
- 2 cups cracked ice

1. To prepare the garnish, cut the cucumber in half lengthwise. Trim off the ends; scoop out and discard the seeds. Cut the halves into quarters, then into eighths, creating sticks about 3 inches long. One cucumber yields approximately a dozen sticks.

2. In a blender, combine all the ingredients except the cucumber sticks. Blend until thick and slushy, with no ice chips remaining.

3. Divide the mixture among four 6-ounce cocktail glasses. Garnish each drink with a cucumber stick.

Serves 4

Brazilian sugarcane coffee shake

Call it the samba of milk shakes: a marching band of percussive flavors that will fire up the hips and make you want to dance on tabletops. Whatever you call it, this much is sure: it will give a whole new spin to your burger and fries (don't bring us down with a veggie burger, please). Brazilian cachaca, made from unrefined sugarcane, is on the list at Cocktail Nation head-quarters. Devotees go for its warm, earthy, brandylike bite, with an intriguing character all its own.

- Bittersweet chocolate rim (see page 16)
- 1 1/2 ounces cachaca or light rum
- 1/2 ounce Tia Maria
- 1/2 ounce Triple Sec
- 1/2 cup coffee ice cream
- 1/2 cup crushed ice

1. Prepare a 6-ounce cocktail glass with the bittersweet chocolate rim. Place the glass in the freezer to chill while preparing the drink.

2. In a blender, whirl the cachaca, Tia Maria, and Triple Sec for a few seconds, just enough to combine. Add the coffee ice cream and ice. Blend until thick and smooth.

3. Pour the mixture into the prepared glass and serve.

Serves 1

Pineapple coconut zowee

Forget piña coladas and beach balls in the sand. Gidget has grown up and it's a whole new wave. This dreamy blend of orange-scented, coconut-pineapple froth is what snow in the tropics must taste like. It's ideal for backyard brunches but just as satisfying while cutting up old photos of exes or calibrating body fat.

- 1 1/4 ounces silver tequila
- 3/4 ounce Cointreau
- 1 ounce canned coconut milk
- 1 1/2 ounces Sweet and Sour (see page 19)
- 1/2 cup fresh pineapple chunks
- 1 1/2 cups cracked ice

GARNISH
- One 2-inch pineapple wedge
- 1 tangerine slice
- 1 peeled kiwi slice

1. In a blender, whirl the tequila, Cointreau, coconut milk, and Sweet and Sour for a few seconds, just enough to blend. Add the pineapple and ice. Blend until the mixture is almost pureed and foamy but without any visible chunks.

2. Pour the drink into a large wine goblet.

3. With a plastic sword toothpick, skewer the pineapple wedge between the tangerine and kiwi slices and pop it into the glass.

Serves 1

Hot as Haiti

It's one of those blistering days, and even when stripped down to the shortest shorts and a threadbare halter you still feel mugged by the heat. Let's not even talk about what this does to the hair. What you need is something more cooling than a convertible ride: a drink to transport you to a state of island bliss, where the sound of the breakers mingles with whispers of palm leaves rustling in the trade winds. We'll leave the cute cabana boy image to you. This drink has all of the sizzle of a sun-drenched vacation, courtesy of cocktail master Scott Bartley.

- Two seeded 1-inch lime wedges
- Two seeded 1-inch tangerine or orange wedges
- 1 tablespoon sugar
- 6 to 8 ice cubes or 1 1/2 cups crushed ice
- 1 ounce good-quality dark rum, such as Barbancourt Haitian
- 3 to 4 ounces chilled ginger brew or ginger ale

1. Place the lime wedges, tangerine wedges, and sugar in the bottom of an 8-ounce double old-fashioned glass or a thick, heavy-bottomed glass.

2. Muddle the mixture until the juice is extracted from the fruit wedges and the sugar is completely dissolved in the juices.

3. Add enough ice cubes or crushed ice to fill the glass. Pour in the rum, and top with the ginger brew to serve.

Serves 1

Pink melon fever

Watermelon is not the kind of fruit you eat alone, and that goes from half-moon, seed-spittin' slices to neat-freak melon balls. This thick, slushy cooler is perfect for a patio soiree at dusk, an impromptu barbecue, or a front porch menu of waffles and gossip — in short, any hot-weather occasion when the only flavor that makes sense is watermelon. Depending on how many of these you have and how well you know your friends, you might find yourself running through the sprinkler in your thong or your muumuu.

- 1 cup crushed ice
- 6 ounces well-chilled lemon vodka
- 3 ounces fresh lemon juice
- 3 ounces sugar syrup (see page 18)
- 4 cups cubed and seeded watermelon

GARNISH
- Six 2-inch watermelon wedges
- 6 green cocktail cherries

1. Put the ice in a blender and pour in the lemon vodka, lemon juice, and sugar syrup. Blend a few seconds until the mixture is somewhere between slushy and chunky. Add the watermelon cubes. Blend until slushy and well combined.

2. Divide the mixture among six 8-ounce wine goblets.

3. With plastic sword toothpicks, skewer each watermelon wedge with a green cocktail cherry and pop one into each drink to garnish.

Serves 6

Surfer girl

Okay, it's a perfect beach day, but unless you've got your own jet, switch to plan B: sip this aquamarine cocktail while bopping to surf music or sobbing over *Baywatch* reruns. It's a heat-whipping, beach-blanket blend, so sharp and crisp you can almost taste the sea breeze. Cut a lemon peel into a surfboard shape for that gnarly summer ride.

GARNISH
- 1 lemon

- 1 1/2 cups cracked ice or 6 ice cubes
- 1 1/2 ounces well-chilled vodka
- 1 ounce Midori (melon liqueur)
- 1 1/2 ounces Sweet and Sour (see page 19)
- 1/4 ounce blue curaçao

1. Chill a 6-ounce martini glass.

2. To prepare the garnish, carefully peel the lemon, keeping large sections of the peel intact. Flatten the peel on a cutting board. With a paring knife, cut the peel into the shape of a surfboard, about 1/2 inch wide and 2 1/2 inches long. When finished, it should be bowed out in the middle with a rounded point at each end. One lemon yields about 8 "boards" or garnishes.

3. Fill a cocktail shaker with the ice and add the vodka, Midori, Sweet and Sour, and blue curaçao. Shake vigorously to blend and chill. Strain the mixture into the chilled glass. Pop a "board" into the drink to garnish.

Serves 1

the bubbles we've seen

You can be schlepping around in pink curlers and satin mules with marabou trim from Sadie's vintage shop or flashing a strapless gown above Manolo Blahnik stilettos. Shabby or chic, hair up or down, sipping Champagne always makes you feel like a million bucks. This is history's most effective romance sparkplug, the ultimate toast, the fizz of the party, the very definition of celebration. Whether you grab a bottle off the grocery rack or special-order one from an exclusive cellar in northern France, add it to our bubbly formulas and dress up any mood.

- **The perfect champagne cocktail**
- **Blushing bride brew**
- **Blame it on Rio**
- **Blood orange mimosa**
- **Power shower punch**
- **All about New Year's Eve**

The perfect champagne cocktail

When Cole Porter sang, "I get no kick from Champagne," he wasn't talking about the bright, toasty cocktail that stands as the symbol of sophistication. But he may have had a point, given all the wimpy stand-ins trying to pass as the svelte, super-crisp, bitter-tinged legend. The ingredients may be simple, but to find true love — a nose-tingling finish that tastes like moonlit silk — it's all in the technique: generously soaking a sugar cube with bitters, then muddling them together to release the mind-snapping essence of bitter and sweet. Splurge on top-flight bubbly, and get ready for the kick of your life.

- 1 sugar cube
- 4 to 5 drops bitters
- 4 to 5 ounces well-chilled Champagne

GARNISH
1 lemon twist

1. Drop the sugar cube into the bottom of a Champagne flute, and pour the bitters on top. Let the cube absorb the bitters until amber-colored — about 30 seconds.

2. Muddle the cube, breaking it up into a soft, granulated mound. Slowly, add half of the Champagne, letting the bubbles rise, then subside. Add the rest of the Champagne, pouring slowly until it just about reaches the top of the glass.

3. Twist the lemon peel over the top and drop it into the drink to serve.

Serves 1

Blushing bride brew

Getting married ranks highest on the occasion meter, given that it happens once in your life (okay, twice; all right, *maybe* three times). So why not give the bride and groom a knot-tying tonic they'll never forget? This one arrives with the requisite color of romance, a passionate rose hue. Relish the moment — romance is as ephemeral as an autumn sunset. Five years from now, he'll be telling you for the fifth time to pop him a beer before half-time.

- 2 frozen raspberries
- 1 1/2 cups cracked ice or 6 ice cubes
- 1 ounce cranberry juice
- 3/4 ounce fresh lime juice
- 1/2 teaspoon sugar syrup (see page 18)
- 1/2 ounce Cointreau
- 1/4 ounce Chambord
- 6 to 8 ounces well-chilled Champagne

GARNISH
- 2 lime twists

1. Place one frozen raspberry in each of two Champagne flutes.

2. Fill a cocktail shaker with the ice and add all the ingredients except the Champagne and the garnish. Shake vigorously to blend and chill.

3. Strain the mixture evenly between the flutes. Slowly add enough of the Champagne to fill the glasses, but do not stir. Twist a lime peel over each drink, then drop it into the flute to serve.

Serves 2

Blame it on Rio

We lowered the neckline, bared the midriff, and fashioned the Champagne cocktail into instant Ipanema. Golden and playful, it's the perfect break from a bleak day: part Carnaval and part bossa nova, with the spicy bite of Brazilian cachaca and the sensual undertones of banana liqueur. Draw the shades, crank up the thermostat, put on that sarong, and conjure up the sound of the surf, not to mention the duty-free shops.

- 2 sugar cubes
- 4 to 6 drops orange bitters
- 1 1/2 cups cracked ice or 6 ice cubes
- 1/2 ounce cachaca or light rum
- 1 ounce crème de banane
- 6 to 8 ounces well-chilled Champagne

1. Divide the sugar cubes between two Champagne flutes, placing each in the bottom of the glass. Douse each cube with orange bitters and set aside.

2. Fill a cocktail shaker with the ice and add the cachaca and crème de banane. Shake vigorously to blend and chill.

3. Strain the mixture and divide it evenly between the prepared flutes. Slowly add enough of the Champagne to fill the glasses, but do not stir. Serve immediately.

Serves 2

Blood orange mimosa

It's not just for breakfast anymore. Fresh orange juice works great any time of the day, especially when fused with Champagne and the intoxicating tang of tangerine. Add some juice from a blood orange, an exotically sweet variety with dazzling ruby flesh. And there you have it — an updated classic so expressive and complex it may require a follow-up session with your shrink.

- 2 ounces fresh blood orange juice, strained
- 2 ounces fresh tangerine juice, strained
- 6 to 8 ounces well-chilled Champagne

GARNISH
- 2 spiraling blood orange peels (see page 15)

1. Combine the blood orange and tangerine juice and divide the mixture between two Champagne flutes.

2. Slowly add enough of the Champagne to fill the glasses, but do not stir.

3. Drop a blood orange spiral into each drink to garnish.

Serves 2

Power shower punch

This punch has quite the zing and all the elements to giggle up a serious suit crowd or the Addams Family relatives. Steer the mood away from the painfully feigned oohs and ahs as you unwrap cousin Clampett's green shag bathroom rug shaped like a giant foot. Choreographed with citrus notes, cheeky blackberry, and earthy almond moves, this intricate punch should spice any conversation and make your guests feel special. A few of these and they might even talk you out of marrying what's-his-name. After all, what are friends for?

- 3 ounces fresh lime juice
- 4 ounces fresh lemon juice
- 5 ounces fresh tangerine or orange juice
- 2 ounces sugar syrup (see page 18)
- 10 ounces pineapple juice
- 5 ounces good-quality brandy
- 5 ounces crème de cassis
- 1 ounce Amaretto
- One 750-ml bottle well-chilled Champagne

1. In a large punch bowl or two pitchers, combine all the ingredients except the Champagne. Refrigerate at least 1 hour or until well chilled.

2. Slowly add the chilled Champagne and serve in 4-ounce punch cups.

Serves 12

VARIATIONS For a bridal shower, garnish with floating citrus-peel knots (see page 15); for a baby shower, float multicolored cocktail cherries like balloons.

All about New Year's Eve

As the clock's winding down on another year, crack up with a cocktail study of Monet's garden — colorful edible flowers floating in a lush pastel wash of pomegranate hues. If there's a drink meant to celebrate the art of life, this is it, courtesy of our Champagne guru, Jeanne Subotnick. Fasten your seat belts, it's going to be a bubbly night.

- Two 750-ml bottles well-chilled Champagne
- 1 fifth of brandy
- 10 ounces pomegranate concentrate juice or Grenadine Pomegranate Syrup (see Note)
- 1 quart chilled sparkling soda water

GARNISH
- Floating edible flowers, such as rose petals, pansies, and nasturtiums

© Bettmann/CORBIS

1. In a large, chilled punch bowl or two large pitchers, combine all the ingredients except the garnish.

2. Float the flowers on top and serve immediately in 4-ounce punch cups.

Serves 40

NOTE: Pomegranate concentrate juice can be found in Middle Eastern or specialty food stores; Trader Vic's Grenadine Pomegranate Syrup is widely available in liquor stores and upscale supermarkets.

Chapter 7

I dream of martinis

The heart of the new cocktail movement is the advent of wild vodka martinis. The classic martini was an icon of the '50s, a man's club drink built on gin and vermouth, rocket fuel and skinny ties, crooning and the dawn of fashionable cynicism. Then came the late-century girls, full of new-found attitudes and their own ideas about martini art: start with good vodka, add anything delicious, different, or daring, and package it with rims or garnishes as bold and sublime as a Georgia O'Keeffe flower. For purists who can't cut loose in our brave new world of recipes, we offer the classic Boy Toy Martini. But if you can come out and play, these new kids on the rocks will be friends forever. Many of these drinks call for flavored vodkas, available in liquor stores, though homemade versions are fantastic (see page 20).

- **Boy toy martini**
- **Babe de-luxe chocolatini**
- **Chai martini**
- **Pomegranate planet martini**
- **XXpresso martini**
- **Tokyotini**

Boy toy martini

Lose the anything-goes 'tude and tune into the male obsession with the martini ritual. Vodka, or, good grief, *flavored* vodka, is tantamount to dragging him to the mall for three hours or serving petit fours at his Super Bowl party. Don't mess with the prototype: use the best gin, keep the vermouth lean and everything numbingly cold — from the shot glass to the liquor. Do not even mention the "shake" word. Instead, stir like a Kung Fu master walks: without making a sound. Ask knowingly if he'd like a lemon twist. Make this one right and you'll be stirred — but he'll be shaken.

- 3 ice cubes
- 2 pitted green olives
- 2 teaspoons dry vermouth, preferably Noilly Prat
- 1 1/2 cups cracked ice
- 3 ounces chilled top-quality gin, such as Bombay Sapphire or Tanqueray

1. Rinse a martini glass with cold water, fill with ice cubes, and place in the freezer for 5 to 10 minutes to completely chill.

2. Meanwhile, spear the olives with a toothpick. Pour the vermouth into a small saucer. Add the olives and turn several times to coat with the vermouth. Let stand for 5 minutes.

3. Fill a cocktail shaker with the cracked ice. Drain the vermouth from the olives and add it to the shaker. Then add the gin. With a long-handled bar spoon, stir very gently to chill, about 15 times in a clockwise direction. Or just swirl the gin in the shaker until chilled. Either way, work quickly so the ice doesn't melt and dilute the gin.

4. Remove the glass from the freezer and discard the ice cubes. Set the speared olives in the martini glass. Strain the gin over the olives and serve.

Serves 1

Babe de-luxe chocolatini

Sometimes you can't be the perfect woman, surviving on rice cakes and working those office memos until 10 P.M. every night. Rinse away that stiff facade with a touch of unbridled decadence. We're not just talking about the standard sweet fix or "Hoover-ing" that box of chocolates but a taste of the outrageous: a voluptuous, bronzed-hued cocktail gloriously rimmed in cocoa and sugar. It fits any occasion — bachelorette parties, after-dinner indulgences, midnight sorties, or just when you need to loosen up more than your joints.

- Cocoa-sugar rim (see page 17)
- 1 1/2 cups cracked ice or 6 ice cubes
- 1 1/2 ounces chilled Mandarin vodka
- 1 ounce Godiva liqueur
- Splash of Grand Marnier

1. Rim a martini glass with the cocoa-sugar mixture, then chill the glass.

2. Fill a cocktail shaker with the ice and add the Mandarin vodka, Godiva liqueur, and Grand Marnier. Shake vigorously to blend and chill.

3. Strain the mixture into the prepared glass and serve.

Serves 1

Chai martini

Call it Zen and the Art of Martini Maintenance. This is East Indian
chai culture rediscovered, a meditation on the ancient silk trade routes,
a way to levitate your karma in case you were no more than a dry
martini in your past life. Don't ask what it all means, just trust us,
it's happening. Your call: a few enlightened sips of this vanilla-clove-
orange-scented black tea cocktail or three hours in yoga class.

- 1 1/2 cups cracked ice or 6 ice cubes
- 1 1/2 ounces chilled vanilla vodka
- 1 1/2 ounces chilled chai tea concentrate (see Note)
- 1 ounce orange liqueur, such as Harlequin or Cointreau

GARNISH
- 1 spiraling orange peel (see page 15)

1. Fill a cocktail shaker
with the ice and
add all the
ingredients
except the
garnish.
Shake
vigorously to
blend and chill.
Strain the mixture into a 6-ounce
martini glass.

2. Drop the spiral in the middle of the
drink and serve.

Serves 1

NOTE: Chai tea concentrate is available in many specialty food stores and coffee
outlets. If unavailable, substitute black tea strongly brewed with a few cloves
and cardamom seeds, a little honey, and a cinnamon stick.

Pomegranate planet martini

This drink shimmers like rubies in the night sky, a hue so saturated with deep crimson translucence that it could be framed and put in a museum. The color comes by way of pomegranate juice, also the source of fruity intensity. A few sips and you'll be singing "Lucy in the Sky with Pomegranates" and toasting the drink's savvy creator, Rebekah Alden.

- 1 1/2 cups cracked ice
- 2 ounces chilled vodka
- 1 to 2 teaspoons pomegranate concentrate juice or Grenadine Pomegranate Syrup (see Note)
- 1 teaspoon fresh lemon juice
- 1 1/2 teaspoons sugar syrup (see page 18)

1. Chill a 4-ounce cocktail glass.

2. Fill a cocktail shaker with the ice and add the remaining ingredients. Shake vigorously to blend and chill. Taste and adjust the amount of pomegranate flavor.

3. Strain the mixture into the glass and serve.

Serves 1

NOTE: Pomegranate concentrate juice can be found in Middle Eastern or specialty food stores; Trader Vic's Grenadine Pomegranate Syrup is widely available in liquor stores and upscale supermarkets.

XXpresso martini

Here's a new twist on getting wired, girl-style. Three-martini lunches are out, but there's no reason why you couldn't slide one of these down and still write that 10-point mission statement, throw together a kick-ass stir-fry dinner, pop into a few chat rooms, and knit a sweater. This road-tested buzz ride won't let you down.

- Turbinado sugar rim or sugar rim (see page 17)
- 1 1/2 cups cracked ice or 6 ice cubes
- 1 1/2 ounces chilled coffee vodka
- 1 ounce espresso or strong coffee
- 1/2 ounce Kahlua
- 1/2 ounce white crème de cacao

1. Sugar the rim of a 6-ounce martini glass and chill the glass.

2. Fill a cocktail shaker with the ice and the remaining ingredients. Shake vigorously to blend and chill.

3. Strain the mixture into the prepared glass and serve.

Serves 1

Tokyotini

This swank, sake-splashed concoction has a lemon-ginger edge that can knock the sash off your kimono. Like relationships, it is at once simple and complex, sweet and tart, with a candied ginger garnish that is pure conversational poetry. Call up a few girlfriends, and order in a bunch of sushi (don't forget: extra wasabi!); multiply the cocktail proportions as needed. Then sip, nibble, and indulge in group Internet shopping while invoking the spirit of our martini haiku:

> *I sip the liquids.*
> *Out comes the charge cards*
> *Stores closed. I order online.*

- Powdered sugar rim (see page 17)
- 1 1/2 cups cracked ice or 6 ice cubes
- 1 1/2 ounces chilled lemon vodka
- 1/2 ounce sake
- 1 1/2 teaspoons ginger syrup (see page 18)
- 2 tablespoons fresh lemon juice

GARNISH
- One 3/4-inch-long piece candied ginger

1. Chill a 4-ounce cocktail glass. Just before assembling the drink, powder the rim with sugar, and set aside.

2. Fill a cocktail shaker with the ice, lemon vodka, sake, ginger syrup, and lemon juice. Shake vigorously to blend and chill.

3. Strain the mixture into the prepared glass. Make a slit in the middle of the candied ginger and slide it onto the rim to garnish.

Serves 1

Chapter 8

party girls

Girls have always outscored their male competitors on the social index. Any third-grade playground is spotted with clusters of girls having fun: whispering the latest line, jump-rope chanting, or giggling up a storm. Guys are in sparse, intense groups arguing over who gets to feed the potato bug to the spider. Let's face it: girls have the upper hand in the get-together universe — they only need two people and one little occasion to kick off a happening. The following repertoire will take you from August weekend blowouts to winter holiday bashes, certain to turn a snoozy stand-around into a soiree of unforgettable decibels.

- **Girls just wanna have rum**

- **Blissed out blackberry-pineapple daiquiri**

- **Carmen Miranda sangria**

- **Eggnog of the party goddess**

- **Pink poodle**

- **Anti-Super Bowl punch**

Girls just wanna have rum

It started with rum and Coke and that first fraternity party where your best friend locked herself in the bathroom with the date who was supposed to be with *you*. The next move was to drop the pop, take it straight to the dance floor, and discover the rumba.

Rum, relationships, and dancing seem to create a stir whenever they meet. The action gets even better when you jettison the jerks (both of them) and concentrate on exotic combos and contagious grooves. Cocktail wizard Jeanne Subotnick gives this jumping number a purple haze and lime perfume. Multiply proportions to fit the crowd.

- 5 ice cubes
- 3 ounces dark sweet rum, such as Gosling's Black Seal
- $1/2$ ounce cassis
- 2 to 3 teaspoons fresh lime juice, strained
- $1^1/2$ ounces chilled cranberry juice

GARNISH
- 1 lime wedge

1. Put the ice in an 8-ounce double old-fashioned glass. Add all the ingredients except the garnish.

2. Squeeze the lime over the top. Give a quick stir, drop the lime into the glass, and serve.

Serves 1

Blissed out blackberry-pineapple daiquiri

Can't afford a spa? Here's the next best thing: an instant mind massage. It's like biting into a fresh-picked berry — heavenly and jolting and high summer all at once, with enough vitamins to offset any guilt. But what transports this deep-pink drink to the realm of the Fifth Element is pineapple-infused rum.

- 5 cups crushed ice
- 9 ounces pineapple-infused rum (see page 21)
- 6 ounces Chambord
- 6 ounces fresh lime juice
- 3 ounces fresh lemon juice
- 5 ounces sugar syrup (see page18)

GARNISH
- 6 pineapple wedges
- 12 fresh raspberries

1. Put half of the ice in a blender and add half of the remaining ingredients except the garnish. Blend until well combined and slushy. Repeat the process to make a second batch.

2. Divide the mixture among six 6-ounce wine goblets. With a plastic toothpick, skewer a pineapple wedge between two raspberries and decorate the rim of a goblet; repeat the process to garnish the remaining goblets.

Serves 6

Carmen Miranda sangria

This is proof that opposites attract. Take some heady Spanish red wine and amplify it beyond the standard sangria formula with the smoky elegance of Cognac. To this suave canvas, add the wild sunrise of tropical flavors: the pale orange of papaya, the yellow shimmer of star fruit, the creamy white of bananas. It's a vibrant union, on loan from sangria maven Liliane Downing, inspired by years on the Costa Brava, and best celebrated with a bunch of friends.

- 2 oranges, sliced
- 1 lemon, sliced
- 2 bananas, peeled and sliced
- 1 papaya, peeled, seeded, and cubed
- 1 star fruit, sliced
- $1/4$ cup sugar syrup (see page 18)
- $1^1/2$ ounces Cognac
- $1^1/2$ ounces Cointreau
- 2 cinnamon sticks, broken into small pieces
- Two 750-ml bottles dry Spanish red wine
- Approximately 6 cups ice cubes

1. In a large (at least 2-liter) glass pitcher, combine the fruit.

2. Add the sugar syrup, Cognac, Cointreau, and cinnamon sticks, stirring gently with a long-handled wooden spoon to combine. Gently stir in the wine.

3. Refrigerate for at least 1 hour to chill.

4. Serve in wine goblets or glasses filled with ice cubes.

Serves 10

Eggnog of the party goddess

Straight from the dining room of paradise, this capricious combo frees the old egg from its retro shackles with a wild side fit for hip chicks. Forget slaving over the whipped egg yolks. Just buy the nog, and take it to the moon with Baileys Irish Cream. Then spend the extra time fretting over the arch of your eyebrows. Rearrange the furniture, sweep everything into the nearest drawer, and get your hip holiday music selection in order.

- 1 1/2 quarts eggnog
- 16 ounces Baileys Irish Cream
- 10 ounces bourbon
- Fresh nutmeg for grating or ground nutmeg for dusting

1. In a large saucepan, heat the eggnog over low heat until steam rises from the surface; do not boil.

2. When the eggnog is hot, remove the pan from the heat and stir in the Baileys and the bourbon.

3. Serve in 6-ounce punch cups or heatproof mugs, with a little nutmeg freshly grated or sprinkled on top.

Serves 12

Pink poodle

This is drink made for a post-modern all-girl sock-hop, a gathering of best buds with a wacky sense of a humor, a passion for thrift-store scores and fingernail polish, and a yen for grinding out the Swim, the Watusi, and the Shimmy-Shimmy Shake on the living room carpet. Get the night rolling with this trashy-chic cocktail that would even get Fifi dancing on her hind legs. Woof.

- Pink coconut rim (see page 17)
- 3 cups cracked ice or 12 ice cubes
- 1 1/4 cups dark rum
- 1 cup cream of coconut
- 2 cups half-and-half
- 3 ounces grenadine
- 1 tablespoon pure vanilla extract

1. Rim 6 cocktail glasses with the pink coconut, then chill the glasses until ready to serve.

2. In a blender, combine half of the remaining ingredients. Blend until all the ice chunks are smooth. Divide the mixture evenly between 3 of the prepared glasses and serve.

3. Repeat the process with the remaining ingredients to create 3 additional drinks.

Serves 6

CHEZ WHEN!

Anti-Super Bowl punch

During that annual midwinter male disorder known as Super Bowl Sunday, you could be having a nervous breakdown on the other side of the couch and still be unable to compete with a third and long (whatever *that* is). Our advice: blow this joint. Get a group of similar seasonal rejects together, grab your guy's favorite chip bowl on the way out, and fill with punch boasting more action than a hundred-yard kickoff return (whatever *that* is). Serve with apples cut into football shapes floating on top — a spoof almost as fun as snickering at the half-time cheerleaders (whatever *they* are).

- 1 apple, halved, cored, and seeded
- Ground cinnamon
- 3 tablespoons brown sugar
- 3 tablespoons softened butter
- $1/2$ teaspoon each ground cloves, cinnamon, cardamom, and nutmeg
- 3 cups apple cider
- $1^1/2$ cups dark rum
- $1^1/2$ cups half-and-half

GARNISH
- 8 to 10 cinnamon sticks

1. To make football-shaped apples, cut the apple halves into again. Cut each quarter in half, for a total of eight thick apple slices. Round off each slice with a diagonal cut at the tip ends to make a football or almond shape. Dust each "football" with a little cinnamon and set aside.

2. In a small bowl, cream the brown sugar, butter, and spices. Set aside.

3. In a large pot, heat the cider until steam rises from the surface; do not boil. Add the sugar-butter mixture, stirring vigorously to dissolve. Reduce the heat to low and simmer for a few minutes; remove from the heat and cool a little before stirring in the rum and half-and-half.

4. Pour the mixture into a large punch bowl or chip bowl. Float the apple shapes on top. Serve in 4-ounce heatproof mugs with cinnamon sticks for stirring.

Makes 8 to 10 servings

Chapter 9
mocktail nation

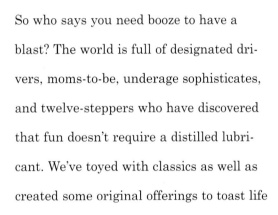

So who says you need booze to have a blast? The world is full of designated drivers, moms-to-be, underage sophisticates, and twelve-steppers who have discovered that fun doesn't require a distilled lubricant. We've toyed with classics as well as created some original offerings to toast life on its own terms.

- **Like a Virgin Mary**
- **Sleepover slammer**
- **Mary Jane**
- **Chinese tea soda with kumquat ice cubes**
- **Ginger-lime snap**

Like a Virgin Mary

Here's the archetypal alcohol-free Bloody Mary, reborn as a garden in a glass. Fresh cucumbers and juicy yellow tomatoes give new life to the traditional tang of Tabasco, lime, garlic, and horseradish. Even before you hit the garnish, you'll feel blushed for the very first time.

- Salt rim (see page 17)
- 1 1/2 ounces fresh lime juice
- 1/2 cup peeled, cubed, and seeded cucumber
- 1 garlic clove, chopped
- 1 teaspoon white horseradish
- 3 to 5 dashes Worcestershire sauce
- 3 to 5 dashes Tabasco sauce
- 2 ounces V-8 or tomato juice
- 1/2 medium yellow tomato, skinned, seeded, and chopped
- 4 or 5 ice cubes

GARNISH
- 1 lime wedge
- 1 cucumber slice

1. Salt the rim of a highball glass and chill the glass.

2. In a blender, thoroughly combine the lime juice, cucumber, garlic, and horseradish. Add the Worcestershire, Tabasco, V-8 juice, and yellow tomato chunks. Blend for a few seconds, just enough to combine.

3. Fill the chilled glass with the ice cubes and add the blended mixture.

4. Squeeze the lime wedge over the drink and drop it into the glass. Make a slit in the cucumber slice and slide it onto the rim to garnish.

Serves 1

Sleepover slammer

It's 11 P.M., you're in the middle of your second video, when a full-blown sweet craving hits. Satisfy your urge without having to rummage for those control-top pantyhose the next morning. Whip up a batch of these rosy, low-fat, fruity-creamy drinks, designed with just enough tang to make your taste buds dance. The formula comes from committed night owl and smoothie operator Clara Eltman.

- ½ cup chopped strawberries
- ⅔ cup orange juice
- 1 cup cracked ice
- ⅓ cup chopped kiwi
- ⅓ cup sliced ripe banana
- ½ to ⅔ cup frozen vanilla yogurt

GARNISH
- 2 strawberries
- 2 peeled kiwi slices
- 2 banana slices

1. In a blender, combine the strawberries, orange juice, and ice until smooth. Blend in the kiwi and banana. Add the yogurt, a scoop at a time, to achieve the desired level of creaminess and thickness.

2. Divide the mixture among two 8-ounce glasses.

3. Place one strawberry, kiwi slice, and banana slice on a plastic sword toothpick. Repeat the process with the remaining fruit. Pop a spear into each drink to garnish.

Serves 2

Mary Jane

Reminiscent of those mythical fountain drinks, this version will inspire you to put on your classic strap-across-the-middle shoes and sip loudly through a straw while twirling your hair. This is pure adolescent flash-back, right down to the innocent fusion of choco-late, peppermint, and seltzer. And you were right . . . you always will be 17.

- 1/4 cup chocolate syrup
- 1 teaspoon peppermint extract
- 2 teaspoons malt powder
- 2 ounces half-and-half
- 6 to 9 ice cubes
- 3 to 4 ounces seltzer

GARNISH
- 1 cherry
- 1 fresh mint sprig

1. Chill a 10-ounce glass.

2. Pour the chocolate syrup, peppermint extract, malt powder, and half-and-half into the bottom of the glass. Stir to combine.

3. Fill the glass to the brim with the ice cubes. Top with the seltzer, then stir gently to combine.

4. Pop a cherry and mint sprig on top to garnish. Serve with a straw and sip from the bottom.

Serves 1

Chinese tea soda with kumquat ice cubes

Here, we've combined the pungent intensity of iced black tea, the sweet aroma of citrus syrup, and the effervescence of charged water with the visual pop of orange kumquats frozen in ice cubes. This freewheeling use of ancient ingredients would puzzle Confucius. But trust us — even he would ask for seconds.

- 1¹/₂ cups strongly brewed black tea
- 20 to 25 kumquat ice cubes (see page 14)
- 8 ounces orange syrup (see page 19)
- 12 ounces sparkling water

1. Refrigerate the tea until chilled — at least a couple of hours.

2. Fill four 10-ounce Collins glasses with the kumquat ice cubes. Layer each glass with 3 ounces of the tea and 2 ounces of the orange syrup. Top each drink with enough sparkling water to almost reach the rim.

3. Stir with a long-handled spoon and serve.

Serves 4

Ginger-lime snap

You've had one too many middle-managers step on your feet today, which were already paralyzed by those pointy-toed Italian shoes. Vanity is a cruel master. Time to kick up your feet and recharge. With its tart sizzle and raspberry afterglow, this cooler should rewire your arches and put a beat in your sole.

- 6 to 8 ice cubes
- 2 ounces fresh lime juice
- 1 ounce fresh lemon juice
- $^1/_4$ cup ginger syrup (see page 18)
- Splash of raspberry syrup
- 3 to 4 ounces sparkling water

GARNISH
- One $^1/_2$-inch-long piece candied ginger
- 2 raspberries

1. Fill a 10-ounce glass with the ice cubes. Add the lime juice, lemon juice, and ginger syrup. Stir with a long-handled spoon to blend.

2. Add a splash of raspberry syrup and top the drink with the sparkling water. With a plastic sword toothpick, skewer the candied ginger between the raspberries and pop into the drink to garnish.

Serves 1

Index alphabetical

Index by ingredients

Acknowledgments

Shakers exploded with ice rocketing against frosted stainless steel walls. Blenders whirred and hissed. Tasters sipped, swished, and pondered each taste nuance. Friends and family pored over recipes, wondering if a shake of chocolate liqueur, fresh mint, and ice cream really would cure hot flashes. We couldn't have completed this book without their input, along with support from our smooth, savvy, beloved editor Bill LeBlond; his kind and acute assistant Amy Treadwell; and copyeditor Lisa Wolff.

Karen Brooks thanks:

My husband, George Eltman, a giant of inspiration and support, who, like a soul-stirring rum, keeps getting better with age. My parents, Ethel and Alan Fleishman, the very definition of love itself. My brother, Craig Fleishman, and nephews Brett, Jason, and Gavin, the keepers of my heart. Tim Sills, my word soulmate, who makes language dance and sing. Ann Wall Frank, the brilliant satirist, who sparked ideas throughout this book. Jeanne Subotnick, for opening up her killer cocktail collection and revealing the secret to the ultimate Champagne cocktail; and Leland and Crystal Payton for digging up retro treasures. To Suzy Kitman, Nancy Cheek, Diane Morgan, Sara Perry, Trink Morimitzu, Rebekkah Alden, Michael Autry, and Liliane Downing for recipes and brainstorming. And a special toast to Victoria Frey, Peter and Julian Leitner, Maya Brand, and *The Oregonian*.

For Gideon Bosker, an exquisite cocktail is best shared with exquisite company. Thanks to Joanne Day, Margarita Leon, Lena Lencek, and Hollis Pinelli Wilde, for showing me where fine spirits and fine drinks intersect.

Reed Darmon thanks Pammela Springfield, owner of Keep 'Em Flying, for kindly dipping into her vast retro treasure box. And fashion maven Jeffrey Kyle for stylish accessories.

Mittie Hellmich thanks Hudson Pierce-Rhoads, Geoff Rhoads, Karen Von Clezie, Scott Bartley, Bobbie Rhoads, Janet Keating, and Steven Corson and the gang at Portland's Uptown Liquor store for putting their lips and tips on the line.

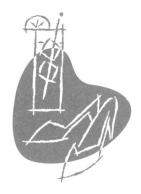